Presented to

_____

Date_____

When Things Go Wrong

BAKER BOOK HOUSE

Grand Rapids, Michigan 49516

Written and Illustrated by
Samuel J. Butcher

Design coordinator
William Biel

Published by Baker Book House
with permission of the
copyright owner

ISBN: 0-8010-0961-8

Printed in USA

To
Ellen Williams
one of my dearest friends

When things go wrong
and we cannot understand,

when life hands us
a big black eye

because we're not prepared
to meet the challenge,

when we are wounded
by the slightest things
that others say

and each day
is just a tale of woe
because

we're caught up
in our problems,

when trials mount

and troubles come

until we're at
the breaking-point

and we cannot
verbalize our thoughts
because it hurts,

when just to be alone
is not enough

and running leads
to nowhere,

then that's the time
when all we need...
is just to have a friend

*whose loving-kindness
reaches out
to lift us up again,*

who will not speak
of butterflies

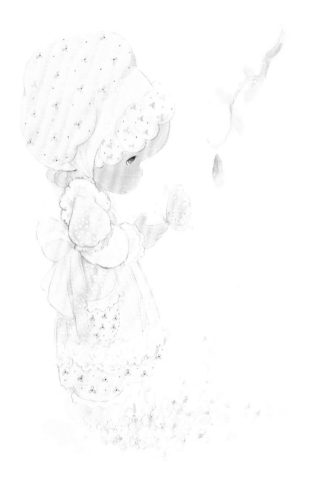

when we feel like a toad

but cautiously
directs our feet

upon a brighter road.

And we know that
all things work together for good
to them that love God, to them
who are the called
according to his purpose.

Rom 8:28